SOARING WITH ST. JOHN:
FLIGHT PATHS OF THE EAGLE

SOARING WITH ST. JOHN

Flight Paths of the Eagle

A Pedagogical Aid

Eugene E. Lemcio

WIPF & STOCK · Eugene, Oregon

SOARING WITH ST. JOHN: FLIGHT PATHS OF THE EAGLE
A Pedagogical Aid

Wipf & Stock
An imprint of Wipf and Stock Publishers
199 W. 8th Ave., Suite 3
Eugene, OR 97401

www.wipfandstock.com

ISBN 13: 978-1-62564-230-1

Manufactured in the U.S.A.

Contents

Abbreviations

AAA	Adopt, Adapt, Arrange (the essential steps in redaction criticism)
AV	Authorized Version
BCE	Before the Common Era
C & D	Cartlidge and Dungan
CE	Common Era
DSS	Dead Sea Scrolls
ET	English Translation
ExpTim	*Expository Times*
FG	Fourth Gospel
FP	Flight Path(s)
GNT	Greek New Testament
HB	Hebrew Bible
HBT	*Horizons in Biblical Theology*
HNTC	Harper's New Testament Commentaries
JSNT	*Journal for the Study of the New Testament*
JSNTMS	Journal for the Study of the New Testament Monograph Series
JTS	*Journal of Theological Studies*
KJV	King James Version
LXX	Septuagint of the Greek Old Testament (=OG)
MT	Masoretic Text of the Hebrew Bible
NETS	New English Translation of the Septuagint
NRSV	New Revised Standard Version
NovT	*Novum Testamentum*
NovTSup	Supplements to Novum Testamentum

NT	New Testament
NTS	*New Testament Studies*
OG	Old Greek (=LXX)
OT	Old Testament
RSV	Revised Standard Version
SG	Synoptic Gospels
SNTSMS	Society for New Testament Studies Monograph Series
STAC	Studies and Texts in Antiquity and Christianity
TynBul	*Tyndale Bulletin*

Definitions

Disciple/ship In the latter half of the twentieth century, this term became generalized and "spiritualized." It lost the significance of the original sense of the Greek and Latin: "student-learner"—a sense that fits well with the revelatory thrust of the Fourth Gospel and with the understanding of Jesus as "Teacher" or "Rabbi."

Dualism A philosophical position that asserts that reality consists of two equal and opposite dimensions, eternally in conflict. Strictly speaking, then, it is inapplicable to phenomena in the Bible, which, were philosophical categories to be applied to it, is fundamentally monistic.

Duality In light of the above, this language is to be preferred when talking about Johannine phenomena such as the tension between good and evil, light and darkness, spirit and flesh, etc.

Eternal Life Literally "life of the age/aeon [to come]"; as defined by Jesus: "to know you the only true God and Jesus Christ whom you have sent" (17:3). The stress is on quality rather than on quantity, as in "everlasting life." In the Fourth Gospel (FG) it is both a present reality (already) and an eschatological/future one (not yet).

Mystery An aspect of human experience that, ironically, is both barrier and gateway, foreclosure and disclosure, prohibition and invitation. In the Bible, it presses towards revelation rather than secrecy. One might call it a mysterious revelation.

Sect(arian) From an ecclesiastical point of view, this has been applied to groups who refuse any longer to be subordinate to the dominant religious authority to which they had once submitted. It is not simply a synonym for an alienated, marginalized body whose ideas and practices are designed to exclude.

Preface

THIS IS THE THIRD work of an informal "series" that seeks to provide an aid for classroom teaching and learning at the university and seminary level. "Charts," "maps," and now "flight plans" are meant to help instructors and students to see relationships among elements of the Fourth Gospel—similarities as well as differences, both internally (within and among chapters) and externally (with regard to the Gospel's various environments). The aim is to display visually as well as to investigate verbally.

Employing the imagery of flight taps into the longstanding tradition within the church of symbolizing John's Gospel pictorially by the eagle—whose imagery has been expounded so effectively in recent years by Richard Burridge in his book *Four Gospels, One Jesus?* (as before, I shall use abbreviated internal citations, with a complete list of works cited in the Bibliography). However, using airborne and aviary imagery can be risky business. As is true generally, one must be careful about pressing any metaphor beyond a certain point. They do not "crawl on all fours." For example, the language of "soaring" might convey the sense of escape, withdrawal, or flights of fancy—of being "above it all." Worse still, in the case of eagles, one may be tempted to think of secluded, elevated aeries where the raptor deposits the "innocent" unsuspecting prey—having been snatched suddenly and taken aloft (out of both sight and mind) by talons hardly touching the surface of soil or water.

Positively, one might stress the advantage of getting a bird's-eye view of the lay of the land, of seeing the forest as well as the trees. Then there is the "eagle eye" that can spot the smallest detail—even at night. Such perspective provides balance and enables the flier to see relationships among the various terrains: water, mountains, valleys, and forests. Literarily, this means viewing a particular text in relation to its various contexts. When this is done, even the so-called Golden Verse (3:16) can appear in a fresh (and, for some, disturbing) light. But such an approach also helps to highlight other relations: that between John and his environment, both biblical and non-biblical (Jewish as well as Greco-Roman). Some of the flight paths make it easier to see how he adopted shared terminology, adapted common ideas, and arranged them (AAA)—in a word, "redacted" them—to suit his purpose(s).

Having said this, I do not want to give the impression that everything potentially visible from "above" has therefore been dealt with in this book. As in the previous volumes, although virtually every chapter has been touched upon, gaps occur, thereby suggesting a lack of completeness and comprehensiveness so far as the entire FG is concerned. Not every topic that could (or should) be covered has been included. And I recognize that not even all aspects of the primary subject of revelation (see below for the justification of this choice) will have been treated—at least not to everyone's satisfaction. In part, this is a practical matter, as the Evangelist himself recognizes at 21:25. One has had to choose from an overabundance of material! So I have settled for being illustrative and paradigmatic rather than exhaustive (and exhausting).

However, there is another reason for being selective. It has to do with encouraging both teacher and student to "Go and do likewise!" for those areas that s/he may feel have been completely ignored at worst or underrepresented at best. My aim is akin to pushing fledglings out of the nest to try their own wings. As in the previous two volumes, where charts and maps have been employed, I regard the FPs primarily as guides to instructing and studying—as means, not as ends. They are not the same as the experience of flying nor the purpose of it (just as the menu should not be confused with the meal, the map not to be regarded as the journey). Such an approach encourages creativity, allowing both teacher and student to chose, modify, and (re)arrange the models, questions, and observations provided.

With such flexibility in mind, I have nevertheless tried to deal with materials according to the sequence of the Gospel. But this has been anything but linear in any rigid sense. For example, some of the FPs—embracing a scope of several chapters—interrupt the narrative progress. However, as Richard Burridge points out, "The flight of the eagle is very complex, soaring up and swooping down, moving forwards and backwards on the winds of the Spirit. . . ." Perhaps this is a good place to remind modern teachers, students, and the general reader that there are various kinds of order, depending on what the user intends to achieve. Thus, chronological order is the province of historians, scientists, and police, for whom establishing the exact sequence of events—as they happened—is essential. Rhetoricians arrange arguments and information to persuade and inspire. Pedagogy and study require presentation and mastery of a subject according to a certain orderliness—which may differ among teachers and learners, depending on personality and content. (However, getting oneself dressed demands a certain order of steps: socks (always) before shoes, etc.) Literary order may have several, simultaneous goals: providing a theological or christological point of view ("According to John"), conveying information, persuading, inspiring, and giving pleasure.

Such study belongs primarily to a version of literary criticism—the first, most basic step of all criticism. The text as it stands supplies the hardest evidence available. (Reading that which appears on the lines should necessarily precede reading between them.) Other "histories" follow: redaction history, form and tradition history, and (finally) the historical reconstruction of original events and sayings. In this way, the text may be kept from the endangered species list. All too often, it becomes ignored when mined as a source for reconstructing history—be that the history of Jesus or the history of the communities who preserved the traditions that the author assembled into their final form. (Of course, I am not suggesting that such research is inappropriate. Rather, my point is that this kind of investigation should be a secondary or tertiary enterprise.) Furthermore, employing the Gospel as a resource for further theological reflection is not to be denied, either. Again, it is a matter of first things first.

Once the literary priority is established, how should one proceed to determine the major theme(s) that the FPs will treat? Although there are hazards in the approach, noticing frequency of usage is the most objective tack to take. Which terms and ideas are most often employed? In this instance, quantity is an indicator of quality. Furthermore, that which appears in the introduction (if it really "introduces") alerts the reader to those subjects that will be developed more fully in the body of the text. So far as the dominant theme is concerned, it is common to see John's as the Gospel of Life, a topic that that author introduces straightaway. Moreover, its frequency and occurrence at crucial instances merit such a conclusion.

However, there is another category that, by these same criteria, requires consideration—and this not only because of the numerous occurrences of a single word but also by clusters of its synonyms: terms for revelation such as "knowledge," "light," "testimony," "witness," etc. (as FP 4 amply illustrates). Furthermore, they help to answer the question, "How does one acquire life?" Consequently, one way or another, the other FPs endeavor to show how the author of the FG puts his distinctive stamp on an issue that, in various genres and strategies, every NT writer treats.

Having gathered the data according to such principles, I have displayed them with the following considerations in mind. Rather than providing a rigid structure for indoctrination and memorization, the tables (the FPs) accompanied by statements and questions should foster orderly and disciplined instruction and study. The charts are of two kinds: the majority provides data in categories that can be inferred because of their frequency or strategic character (the subjective nature of this judgment being reduced by evidence and argument). Interspersed among them are grids that demonstrate systematic analysis (a taking apart) and synthesis (a putting together) by posing "investigative" questions long used in literature and journalism classes: Who? (Agent; initiator or recipient), What? (Action/Event), When? (Time), Where? (Place), How? (Means/Manner/Method/Instrument), How Far/Many/Much? (Scope/Quantity), What Kind? (Quality), Why? (Purpose/Cause), So What? (Significance), etc.[1]

Using these categories enables analysis and synthesis to be *comprehensive* in the sense that many aspects of a selected narrative can be covered. At the same time, they make it possible for one to detect that which *integrates* the parts. Approaching literature in this way assists students to develop skills in *comparison* (noting similarities) and *contrast* (seeing differences). Furthermore, applying such neutral classification helps to *increase objectivity* and to limit imposing agendas foreign to a text. No rigid sequence needs to be followed when employing the above. They can be freely reordered to achieve the greatest pedagogical effect. However, it is generally good practice to get an idea of the entire context, to see the forest within which individual trees grow, and to survey the lay of the land. Besides providing a sense of the whole from which to interpret the parts, the bird's-eye view enables one to get a feel for proportion—where the emphases lie, what weight is attributed to certain themes.

In addition to leading the reader in comparing and contrasting categories within the text itself (thereby allowing the Evangelist to speak on his own terms and in his own way—the main objective), I provide opportunities for readers to compare and contrast the Gospel with external sources, both canonical and extra-biblical. Examples of the former are of two kinds: (a) the OT Scriptures acknowledged by all Christians and (b) the New Testament. "Extra-biblical sources" refers to Jewish texts such as the Dead Sea Scrolls (DSS) and to Greco-Roman texts such as Cleanthes'

---

1. Many of these categories and procedures are enshrined in Traina.

"Hymn to Zeus"[2] and inscriptions attributing cures to the god Asclepios. This is an attempt to provide for modern readers samples of the literary environment that shaped the religious world of Jesus, John, and the earliest Christians. They enable one to visualize the contrasts and differences (the continuity and discontinuity) between "Athens and Jerusalem."

So far as the remainder of the NT is concerned, I have studiously avoided harmonizing John with other authors. However, in the case of the Synoptic Gospels (SG), some accounts of the same event or teaching are similar enough that the FPs will do double and even triple duty in providing a framework on the basis of which one can subsequently study the others on their own. Consequently, I have included chapter and verse notations in parentheses under the relevant FP titles. Although the focus of attention is St. John's Gospel, several of the studies that follow involve the SG tradition—sometimes represented by St. Mark for the sake of convenience, but in several cases with a fuller reference to Matthew or Luke (or both). Rather than diluting the work and taking away from its distinctiveness by harmonizing, such a move serves to highlight the salient features of the FG by maintaining the integrity of each.

Once again, I have used the NRSV, except in those passages referring to the "son of man" (where I resort to the RSV). I did so principally because this translation has preserved the expression rather than converting it to the generic "human" or "mortal." Although not a title per se, the term retains a certain formal quality, which NT writers exploit when they appropriate it. Such usage is obscured by the NRSV's otherwise welcome efforts to avoid gender specific translation.

When all of this is said and done, it is the instructor of a particular class who bears the responsibility of using these and other tools and techniques to engage in the complex act of pedagogy. Ink on a page cannot teach; nor can literature fulfill literature. The Bible per se is unable to do so. Although notable exceptions might be cited, one needs the help of an agent—as the encounter between Philip and Ethiopian eunuch shows (Acts 8:30–35). The identity of the Servant in Isaiah 53 was not self-evident. According to Luke's first volume, it had taken a special act of the risen Jesus

---

2. I have received written permission from Mohr Siebeck to reproduce the Greek text and English translation of this work in the Appendix. The Bibliography is obviously not exhaustive. Because this tool is meant to engage students (and teachers!) with primary texts before they resort to secondary sources, I have largely avoided referring to the latter in footnotes. Works supporting pedagogy and study of the primary texts are cited internally and listed in the Bibliography.

to open the eyes of the disciples to see in the Scriptures that the Messiah had to suffer (Luke 24:44–46). Closer to home, only after Jesus had been glorified were the disciples able both to remember what their Lord had said and to realize what he had meant by it (John 2:22; 12:16).[3]

---

3. Even an individual's encounter with a Gideon Bible, alone in a motel room, is dependent on someone's putting it there—and, beforehand, another's conveying the Semitic and Greek texts into the receiving language.

1. John Will Be John.
Distinctive Terms & Themes

Categories	Synoptics (A)	John (B)
1. OT background	Daniel 2, 7	Isa 11:1–2, 9; Deut 17:14–20
2. Style	Short sayings	Long discourses
3. Time of ministry	1 year	3+ years
4. Place(s) of activity	Galilee → Judea, Jerusalem (once)	Galilee ←→ Judea, Jerusalem (several)
5. Topic of preaching/teaching	Kingdom of God [KG]	Eternal/aionic life (17:3)
6. Christology	Secret: "Silence! Don't Tell!"	Public: "I am . . ." (several)
7. "Word"	Proclaimed/taught	Incarnated/enfleshed (1:14a)
8. Sonship	Obedient Son of Man	Obedient Son of God (5:17–30)
9. Relation to Jesus	Following	Believing in (but see 5:24 & 12:44)
10. Exorcisms	Many: evidence for KG	None
11. Mighty works	Miracles	Signs
12. Dualities typical of DSS	—	Above—Below
	—	Spirit—Flesh
	—	Now—Later
	—	Truth—Falsehood
	—	Light—Darkness
	—	Good—Evil

Key Ideas (corresponding to
the numbered categories above):

1. For A (and Revelation), these chapters in Daniel supply the "kingdom" and "son of man" categories. How does Dan 12:4 resemble Isa 11:9 (B)? What might John be claiming against this "background?" Is it fair to generalize that the coming era will be characterized by the kingdom of God according to the SG and by the knowledge of God according to the FG?

2. At least in some instances, A might simply be the tips of the icebergs in B.

3. Might the shorter timeline in A reflect a compression of the more extensive ministry in B? The latter figure is arrived at because of the mention of at least three Passover feasts.

4. This would accommodate travel up and down the land—something that is reflected in Jesus' lament over Jerusalem, as reported by Matt 23:37//Luke 13:34.

5. It is vitally important to define terms internally, to the extent possible. In the case of "eternal/aonic life" (lit. "life of the age [to come]"), a distinction should be made from "everlasting life." The latter has to do with quantity, the former (as defined by Jesus in 17:3) with quality. The life of the age to come is supremely relational—intimate knowledge of the Source of all life and the Agent/Bringer of that life. Might A then be referring to a time when such knowing will constitute the "politics" of the era? In FP 11, I attempt to demonstrate (from Mark 10:17–26) that the two categories belong to a collection of interchangeable terms expressing different aspects of the same larger Reality.

6. This reflects, alongside the theme of #5, one of the two most dramatic differences between the two Gospel traditions—which, as FP 11, 20, and 26 attempt to show, can be overdrawn.

7. Regarding B, see FP 5 for a comparison and contrast with biblical and extra-biblical texts. John's claim is unlike anything to be found in the world's religions. What is the difference between "becoming" flesh and "putting on" flesh? "Word" belongs to a cluster of terms that, one way or another, have to do with communication/revelation

(see FP 4). How does Jesus' own statement (unique in all of the Gospels) about the reason for his being born and coming into the world (18:37) fit into this? How does it differ with common (even Christian) perceptions/claims?

8. What is similar in both instances, despite the differences in christological expression? The fuller dynamic of B combines Father and Son in close cooperation and coordination. Do appeals to the sonship of Jesus in the FG normally focus on his *being* Son, or *behaving* as such? What is the significance of each?

9. It is one of the most striking of differences, there being no instances in A of Jesus calling for the crowds or disciples to "believe *in* him." The single exception of Matt 18:6 is limited to a private session with the disciples about children or immature followers. Might the SG writers have thought that believing was too mental or passive a response to Jesus? Of course, the language and phenomenon of following occur in B as well.

10. This is another stunning contrast, in keeping with the phenomenon of #5.

11. Lest the "merely" miraculous of A be seen as an end in itself, the terminology of B encourages one to look beyond the miracle—that to which the sign is pointing, the Signified.

12. It is such duality (not dualism—see the Definitions) that caused interpreters to find in B the influence of later Greek philosophy. However, the discovery of the DSS has shown that at least some Jews (on Palestinian soil, no less) were used to expressing themselves in such categories. This has led some to conclude that the distinctive idiom of B indicates a desire to reach such Jews with the message of/about Jesus.

2. Two "Looks" on the Fourth Gospel

	Old Look	**New Look**
A. When? (date)	c. 175 CE	c. 100 CE
B. Who/m? (demography)	Gentile Christian	Jewish Christian
C. Where? (places)	Fictional	Actual
D. What? (viewpoint)	Greek philosophical "dualism"	Jewish sectarian "duality"

1. Because the "dualistic" language of the FG seemed more indebted to Greek philosophy, and because so many of the place names in the narrative were not at the time known to historians of the region, many (if not most) scholars in the nineteenth and early twentieth centuries had concluded that the author was a Gentile Christian unfamiliar with Palestinian geography. Therefore, the FG must have been written later than the traditional date of the 90s CE and by someone other than an eyewitness, that is, the Beloved Disciple himself.

2. However, several discoveries began undermining these verdicts:

    a. In the mid-1930s, the British paleographer C. H. Roberts identified a papyrus fragment (Rylands, p54) as a portion of John 18:31–33, 37–38 (Jesus' trial before Pilate). Before knowing of its content, he had dated the copy at c. 125 CE, positing that the original must have been composed c. 100 CE. Ironically, p54 remains the earliest text of the NT available.

    b. During WWII, as British bulldozers prepared for Rommel's invasion of the Middle East, evidence turned up (in Jerusalem and elsewhere) that vindicated the author's knowledge of the territory (C).

    c. During the late 1940s, some of the DSS revealed texts using many of the same dualistic categories once thought to be exclusively Greek-philosophical (D).

    d. Thus, one had to infer that the author was a Jewish Christian who was familiar both with Palestinian geography and also with the thought of sectarian Jews (likely the Essenes)—to whom he sought to bear witness about Jesus in their own idiom.

3. However, have these (re)solved the radical difference in Christology (private/public), the main subject of his preaching and teaching (kingdom of God/eternal or aeonic life), and the manner of relating to Jesus (following/believing)? See also FP 1.

4. Look to FP 11, 20, and 26 for possible solutions.

3. Biblical "Backgrounds" to John & the Synoptics (Mark)

	A	B	C	D
	Daniel 2 & 7 (Isaiah 52:7)	**Mark**	**John**	**Isa 11:1–9**
Subject	Kingdom of God	Kingdom of God	Knowledge=	Knowledge
			Eternal life (17:3)	
				Wisdom
				Understanding
			Spirit of Truth	Spirit
Christology	Son of Man	Son of Man	Logos	Root of Jesse

1. Daniel's influence (A) upon Mark and the Synoptic Tradition (B) seems to be as profound as Isaiah's (D) upon John (C).

2. Of course, the authors of both traditions drew widely from the entire biblical canon. But these two OT authors seem to have contributed a disproportionate influence. Jeremiah's anticipation of a New Covenant includes knowledge of the Lord (31:31–34). However, unlike the Isaiah 11 text, the recipients of that knowledge belong to the house of Israel; and no mediator of the Covenant is envisioned. In the final chapter of Daniel, a more universal expansion of knowledge is foreseen during the coming era/age (12:4), however, no mediator of that knowledge is anticipated.

3. In light of Isa 11:9 ("The earth shall be full of the knowledge of the Lord as the waters cover the sea"), what do you expect to be Jesus' role in fulfilling this goal, according to John?

4. At the end of our study, will you agree with Rudolf Bultmann (*Theology of the New Testament*, 2:66) that what is revealed in the FG is that Jesus is the Revealer?

5. See the potential bridge between eternal life and kingdom of God

displayed in FP 11.

6. Robert Southwell (1561–1595), in his poem "A Child, My Choice,"
    captures the spirit of the connection when he writes, "His knowledge
    rules . . . ."

4. Revelatory Terms by Chapter

	1	2	3	4	5	6	7	8	9	10
Know-	2	2	1	2	2	2	5	6		7
Word (1)	4	1		4	2	1	2	6		2
Word (2)			1		1	2		2		
Light	6		5		1			2	1	
Truth	2		1	2	1			7		
Witness	7	1	6	2	12		1	7		1
Sign		3	1	2		4	1		1	1
Manifest	1	1	1				2		1	
Work			2		1				3	2
Do		3	2	4	4	3	3	1	3	1

	11	12	13	14	15	16	17	18	19	20	21
Know-	1	2	4	7	2	2	8		1		1
Word (1)		2		3	4		4	2	2		1
Word (2)		2		1	1		1				
Light	2	6									
Truth				2	1	3	3	3			
Witness		1	1		2			2	2		2
Sign	1	2								1	
Manifest							1				3
Work											
Do	1	2	2	1	3	1	1			1	

1. Can there be any doubt (based on sheer numbers) that revelation is the dominant category in the FG—just as the political dimension (aspects of the "kingdom of God") is in Mark (and the SG)? Which terms are especially prominent? (See the companion volume Lemcio, *Travels with St. Mark*, 1, 17.)

2. However, truth and knowledge are not simply to be spoken or learned; they are to be done/worked. Jesus himself (the Teacher [Revealer] and Lord) reinforces this point when he declares after the foot-washing event, "If you know these things, blessed are you if you are doing them" (13:17).

3. Think of light in terms of illumination. A familiar cartoon shows a figure struggling over a problem for several frames. When he solves it, a light bulb appears above his smiling face.

4. In light of such data, is it accurate to refer to the FG as the "Gospel of Life"—"life" being itself a prominent term? The question cannot be answered on the basis of quantity alone. It needs pursuing further along these lines: What gives birth to life? What is the means of attaining it?

5. Of the ironic nature of this revelation, Gail O'Day writes (p. 31),

    The incongruities and tensions that draw the reader into the text are the means to draw him or her into participation in this vision [of truth], to make him or her "really *see*." The author of such ironies does not create incongruities or oppositions in order to block meaning and comprehension but to intensify meaning and comprehension.

    . . . .

    Despite its apparent attempts to conceal meaning, *irony is a mode of revelatory language*. It reveals by asking the reader to make judgments and decisions about the relative value of stated and intended meanings, drawing the reader into its vision of truth, so that when the reader finally understands, he or she becomes a member of the community that share that vision, constituted by those who have also followed the author's lead. (emphases original)

5. John 1:1–14. In the Beginning Was the Word: Jerusalem & Athens, Faith & Reason

	Genesis 1 (LXX)	John 1	Cleanthes' *Hymn to Zeus* (lines)
1	In the beginning (1)	In the beginning (1–2)	First cause (2)
2	Ἐν ἀρχῇ	Ἐν ἀρχῇ	ἀρχηγέ
3		was the word (1)	you direct universal reason (12)
4		ἦν ὁ λόγος	κατευθύνεις κοινὸν λόγον
5			one ever-existing rational order (21)
6			ἕνα γίγνεσθαι πάντων λόγον
7		the word was God	
8		θεὸς ἦν ὁ λόγος	
9	and God said . . . (3)	all things were made through him/it (3)	we have our origin in you (4)
10	κ. εἶπεν θεός . . .	πάντα δι' αὐτοῦ ἐγένετο	ἐκ σοῦ γὰρ γένος ἐσμέν
11	a living creature (24)	in him/it was life (4)	of all that live (5)

12	ψυχὴν ζῶσαν	ἐν αὐτῷ ζωὴ ἦν	ὅσα ζώει
13	let there be light (3)	the life was the light of humans	[reason] mingling with small lights (13)
14	Γενηθήτω φῶς	ἡ ζωὴ ἦν τὸ φῶς τ. ἀνθρώπων	μειγνύμενος . . . μικροῖς τε φάεσσι
15	lights . . . of the night (16)	the light shines in the darkness (5)	
16	φωστῆρα . . . νυκτός	τὸ φῶς ἐν τ. σκοτίᾳ φαίνει	
17		the world was made by him/it (10)	the whole universe . . . obeys you (7–8)
18		ὁ κόσμος δι' αὐτοῦ ἐγένετο	πᾶς ὅδε κόσμος . . . πείθεται
19		and the word became flesh (14a)	
20		κ. ὁ λόγος σάρξ ἐγένετο	
21		we beheld his glory (14b)	eagerness for glory (27)
22		ἐθεασάμεθα τ. δόξην αὐτοῦ	ὑπὲρ δόξης σπουδήν

1. The discovery of the DSS reinforced observations about the Jewishness of the FG. However, it is still the case that we are dealing with a Hellenized Judaism in the Palestine of Jesus' day. All four Gospels are known to us only in Greek; and the Greek ideas in John are to be found in the thought world of at least some Jews during the period.

2. Although many fragmentary statements corresponding to the Johannine text could be cited from the LXX and pagan literature, my aim was to put alongside the Prologue the two texts whose language is concentrated in correspondingly brief passages (24 verses and 39 lines, respectively). I have provided the Greek word λόγος for "word" because it is sometimes translated as "reason" and so might be missed. The untranslated Greek words allow readers to see how close the vocabulary actually is. *Legein*, the lexical form of the word behind "said" in the LXX Genesis 1 account, is related to the noun *logos*.

3. Although I have relied for the text and translation provided by Johan C. Thom (see pp. 34–39, 40–41), the display is entirely my own. Portions of the *Hymn* can be found in both Barrett and Kee; see the Appendix for the full text.

4. By observing these echoes in language and theme from two foundational sources, do you agree that this fisherman is casting his net as widely as possible to snag people from both the Jewish and the Greco-Roman world? What are the two most distinctive differences between John and these texts? In speaking of "sources," one must not fall into the trap of thinking that conscious borrowing was taking place. Many of the comparable terms and concepts belonged to a shared intellectual and religious environment. They were adapted, adopted, and arranged (AAA) according to memories and experiences of the earthly and risen Jesus.

5. It is easy to see from the hymn that Cleanthes (with other Greeks) regarded reason as a gift of God—an act of grace, Christians would say. Via Logos, Zeus had created the universe. Humans were imprinted with it, enabling them to think rationally about the ordered world and themselves (including moral behavior). Most importantly, they could learn more about God by thinking well about the cosmos and about the divine.

6. St. Augustine said that before he become a Christian he had read all about the Logos in his philosophical studies—except for one aspect of the divine Word (see *Confessions*, Bk. 7, ch. 9, ll. 19–20). This claim by the FG is unique among all of the world's religions.

7. That truth and goodness may be found throughout human experience is a function—Christians have claimed—of common/universal grace. The slogan "All truth is God's truth" was popularized by the philosopher Arthur Holmes. That concept enabled some early Christian theologians to regard Athens and Jerusalem as sister cities. Others found them to belong to different worlds of thought. With whom would you side?

8. Despite this biblical and patristic embrace of *logos*, many Christians throughout the ages have been suspicious of "reason," believing it to be the opposite of faith—the rational being the enemy of the relational, the mind the antithesis of the spirit. Involving the intellect was sure to pour cold water upon warm-hearted religion. However, are not "reasons of the heart" still "reasons"? Is thinking (too much) about one's deepest commitments the problem, or is the real problem thinking poorly about them?

9. What is the importance of starting off with a reference to "the Word"? I ask this because of the tendency for careless readers to substitute "Jesus" at this point—in an effort to find support for his divinity (or deity). Technically speaking, the incarnate Jesus could not have existed as Jesus before the incarnation of the Word. It would be truer to classical Christian doctrine to supply "the Son" at this point because of the association of Word and Son in 1:14b. But doing so, while more correct, would still miss the significance of the author's choice of terms. None of the more familiar titles for Jesus (Lord, Christ, etc.) is chosen here. What does one do with words? What does God do with "the Word"? So, from the get-go, communication/revelation is set forth as the primary category of the Introduction/Prologue of the FG.

6. John 1:17. Translating "Grace & Truth"

	Grace (abstract)	Truth (abstract)
The Law by Moses	No	No
Jesus Christ	Yes	Yes

1. Nearly all commentators regard the Greek definite article at this point as preceding an abstract notion or quality (which the article can do). However, by not translating it, a severe contrast is posed between the two sources of divine revelation.

2. Yet, at 1:14, the same two terms lack the article. This leads one to consider the possibility that St. John intended a more specific emphasis three verses later.

3. The following display suggests that the articular form is getting at ultimacy or supremacy. It recognizes that, because it was *divine* revelation (to which Jesus appeals), there had been expressions of grace and truth before him. Thus, we can translate, "The Law was given by Moses; but the supreme expression of divine grace and the ultimate expression of God's truth came by Jesus Christ." In English, we sometimes change the pronunciation of "the" to achieve this effect.

	Grace	Truth
The Law by Moses	Yes	Yes
Jesus Christ	Greater	Greater

7. John 1:29. The Lamb of God

	Day of Atonement (Leviticus 16)	Days of Atonement
A. Agent	Goat (animal)	Lamb of God (Jesus)
B. Role	Carry	Carry
C. Burden	Sins (plural)	Sin (singular)
D. Frequency	Once annually	Continuously
E. Scope	Israel	World

1. What double shift has occurred in agency (A)? The Passover lamb did not bring about atonement. Its blood, smeared on the doorposts of Israelites, protected their firstborn sons from the destroying angel sent throughout Egypt (Exod 12).

2. What transformation has taken place in the burden borne (C)? Define the world's sin (not sins) according to the context by thinking about the consequences of opposing that which Jesus as God's Word and Son has come to do (1:18).

3. Regarding D, the Greek continuous action needs to be exploited: "the Lamb of God who *is* tak*ing* away the sin of the world." On this reading, can atonement be confined to a single event at the end of Jesus' life—his death?

4. As is often the case in such adaptations, that which was limited to Israel becomes universal (E).

8. John 1:49. Rabbi, Son of God, King of Israel

Deuteronomy	Proverbs	Psalm 2:6–7	John 1:49
King as student (17:14–20)	King as teacher (1:1, 8)		Rabbi/Teacher
		King	King of Israel
		—as Son of God	Son of God
		—as Messiah	Messiah

1. At first glance, this is a strange combination of terms at 1:49. One might ask, "What is wrong with this picture?!" Which expression is the "odd term out"?2. Long before Jesus appeared on the scene, these terms and roles had been associated. According to the Deuteronomic ideal (17:14–20), the king's role was to become an expert in Torah/the Law. By implication, this schooling equipped him for the role of teacher (Prov 1:1, 8).

2. Grouping "Son of God" and "King of Israel" is natural enough, since the king was commonly called "God's Son." When anointed *mashiach/christos* at the beginning of his reign, he was regarded as God's Messiah/Christ (2 Sam 7:14–17 and Ps 2:6–7; see also Andrew's recognition of Jesus as the Messiah/Christ in v. 41.).

3. The narrator also conveniently translates "Rabbi" as "Teacher" (v. 38), thereby ranking this status and role with kingship, sonship, and messiahship. However, does it dilute or diminish the high-powered nature of the latter two? Or do they enhance it? Recall that revelation is the dominant theme of the FG (and note that Jesus twice refers to himself as "Teacher and Lord" in 13:13–14).

4. "Rabbi" literally means "my great one." It belongs to a time when the learned and learning were revered. A version of this near-awe still persists in places such as Ukraine. In the early 1990s, whenever I entered a classroom (whatever the level—grade school, university, or seminary) students stood because a "professor" had entered the room. In this culture, a member of the intelligentsia is held in honor, as one whose education and outlook are vital to the well-being of the people and nation.

5. These appellations are reinforced and expanded throughout the narrative. For example, regarding 5:19–30, C. H. Dodd has pointed to a parable of apprenticeship, where sons learn from their fathers both the trade and the "tricks of the trade" (p. 386 n. 2). Thus knowing the father's business inside and out, the son will one day be able to conduct business on behalf of his father and subsequently convey such information and skill to his own children. On this analogy, Jesus, as Son, is able to exegete (lit. "lead out" [the meaning of]) the Father (1:18) and to do his will.

6. Given these associations at the beginning of the FG, might they inform the meaning of 20:31 at the end of it—that the "signified" (Jesus), to whom the signs point, is none other than the reliable Son of God and Christ, in either role revealing the Father who had sent him?

9. John 1:52 & Genesis 28:10–20. Two Ladders

	Gen 28:10–20	John 1:52
1. Who? (subject)	Jacob	Jesus
2. What? (action)	Heaven opened	Heaven opened
a. Upwards	Angels ascending	Angels ascending
b. Downwards	Angels descending	Angels descending
3. Whom? (object)	The Lord	The Son of Man
4. Where? (place)	Bethel: "House of God" (14)	Galilee
5. So what? (significance)	All nations to be blessed	[with knowledge]

1. Keep in mind that the Greek *angelos* is the usual word for "messenger." "Angel" (secondary for *divine* messenger) often obscures the essential meaning.

2. We are not told what information the messengers in the Genesis passage actually conveyed. However, given the overriding them of the FG, what does their continuous ascending and descending bring about?

3. How does this fit the Father-Son dynamic in the FG?

4. God reiterates to Jacob the promise that he had made to Abraham: that he and his descendants would bless all the nations. However, the nature of that blessing is not specified there. With what (or how) are the nations to be blessed according to the FG (and the background suggested in Isa 11:9)?

5. According to Daniel 7:13–14, the prophet Daniel saw that the son of man figure was granted a kingdom, authority, and glory. With what will Nathaniel see him endowed?

6. Since Jacob renamed the site of the heavenly ladder "Bethel" ("House of God" in Hebrew), what is the implication for its location in John 1? Relate this to the controversy over Jesus' temple-body statement in 2:19–21. Historically, Bethel had rivaled Jerusalem as the center of Israelite worship—temples being the site where God and humans meet.

10. John 2:13–17 & the Synoptics.
The Temple "Cleansing"

(Matt 21:12–13//Luke 19:45–46)

Lev 12:1–8	John 2:13–17	Mark 11:15–19
	Money changers' tables turned (15)	Money changers' tables turned (15)
Doves for poor	Dove sellers (14, 16)	Dove sellers
	Zeal for the Father's house (17)	House → prayer → nations (17)
	Father's house: place of business (16)	Den of robbers

1. It is a scene that makers of movies about the life of Jesus love to film. For once, the mild-mannered, gentle Jesus of popular and Christian fantasy exhibits some emotion—gets angry. However, the point of this passionate demonstration in the temple is lost. So, the specific actions and statements of Jesus require closer attention.

2. As is often pointed out, moneychangers provided an important function. Pilgrims from the Jewish Diaspora would have carried currency bearing the stamp of a Roman emperor on one side and a scene from Greco-Roman myth on the other. Such violations of the second commandment could not be brought into the sacred precincts. So, temple money was needed.

3. Thus, at one level, Jewish leaders were holding fast to the revelation of God through Moses, as expressed in the second commandment forbidding the making of and contact with graven images. However,

they were missing the mark so far as other expressions of the divine will were concerned. According to Leviticus, these birds (along with pigeons) ought to have been priced low enough for the poor to afford when bringing sons to be circumcised and mothers ritually purified.

4. It is in the Johannine account that doves are mentioned twice (v. 14), suggesting a special emphasis. In the second instance, Jesus' remarks about business are addressed to the dove sellers (v. 16). By implication (otherwise why mention doves twice?), Jesus accuses the sellers of doing business instead of providing a service, thereby necessarily overcharging the poor for the very occasion when the physical sign of Israel's covenant relation to God would be carried out.

5. The same was the concern of Mark, albeit more obviously:

   a. Thus, the reference to stealing ("cave of robbers," echoing the words of Jeremiah) needs to be associated with Jesus' overturning the tables of those who sold doves. Here too, Jesus implies their exploitation of the poor.

   b. Furthermore, when Solomon dedicated the temple, he prayed that foreigners would have access to pray alongside the native Israelites (a theme reinforced by Isaiah). However, in Jesus' day they had been denied this. Our Lord thus attempts to restore the original purpose for the place where (as the king had confessed and prophet had predicted) the God whom the heavens cannot contain was pleased to focus his presence so that one and all could have access.

   c. It is worth noting that, as in John (although in reverse order), Mark—alone of the SG—separates the entry into Jerusalem (by a day) from his temple action. After the grand public procession, with its messianic overtones and undertones, Jesus simply looks around and retreats to Bethany with the Twelve (v. 11). He thereby diffuses (and reinterprets?) the expectations imposed upon him.

11. Eternal Life & the Kingdom of God: A Bridge Too Far (1)?

(Matt 19:16–30//Mark 10:17–26//Luke 18:18–30)

	SG (Mark 10)	John 3:3, 5, 15–17
1. Eternal/aonic life	Inherit (17)	Have (15–16)
2. Kingdom of God	Enter (23–25)	Enter (3, 5; see 18:36–37)
3. Salvation	Being saved (26)	Saved (17)

1. We saw in the overview (FP 1) that perhaps the most profound difference between the FG and the SG is their depiction of Jesus' main subject of *public* preaching and teaching: eternal life and the kingdom of God, respectively.

2. The latter expression occurs only in this chapter—twice, *in private*, and at night in the exchange with Nicodemus. Later, Jesus refers to "my kingdom" and accepts Pilate's reference to him as a "king" (18:36–37, respectively). But that is it.

3. In the SG, a man inquires about *inheriting eternal life*. After he fails to comply with the conditions, Jesus, to the astonishment of his disciples, speaks of the near impossibility for the rich to *enter the kingdom of God*. Peter then wonders about the possibility of anyone's being *saved*.

4. Thus, in these Markan and Johannine passages, there is literary evidence for bridging all three terms: "eternal life," "kingdom of God," and "salvation/being saved." They seem to belong to a cluster of concepts making them virtually synonymous. However, it is a matter of emphasis. "The kingdom of God" dominates the SG, whereas the FG prefers "eternal/aonic life." While both appear in Paul's writings, "salvation" terminology prevails.

12. Johannine Eschatology: Realized & Unrealized

		Already	Not yet
3:18	Unbelievers condemned already		
5:25	The hour is coming & now is: dead will live		
5:28			The entombed will come forth to Resurrection: of life & judgment
11:24			"My brother will rise again in the resurrection on the last day."
11:25	"I am the resurrection and the life"		
12:31–33	"Now [Jesus' death] is the judgment of this world."		
12:31–33	"Now [Jesus' death] this world's ruler will be expelled."		
14:3			I will come again & receive you.
16:11	"This world's ruler has been judged."		

1. Central to some Jews' expectation of the end-time was the resurrection of the dead, their judgment, and the elimination of all contrary rule—be that dominion human, satanic, or an unholy combination of both. On these topics, anyway, where does the emphasis lie in the FG—realized (already), futuristic (not yet), or a combination of the two (already and not yet)?

2. In light of certain interpretations of the book of Revelation, what makes Jesus' statements in 12:31–33 (uttered allowed publicly in Jerusalem) particularly striking? If the expulsion of Satan in Revelation 12 is read as occurring between the newborn child's being set on God's throne and the Lamb's death (vv. 5–11), then the theology of the two accounts may not be all that different—although the mode of expression is distinctive.

3. Scholars who rely on the general trustworthiness of the Gospels observe that, with the teachings and actions of Jesus, many of his followers found themselves "betwixt and between" two poles regarding the expected future: fulfilled and unfulfilled. In reference to the SG, some scholars use "inauguration" for the coming of God's kingdom rather than "realization" (although statements such as Matt 12:28// Luke 11:20 should be noted). But they are more ready to employ the latter for John's perspective.

4. C. F. D. Moule argues that the coming of Jesus in the FG refers to his future contact with individuals rather than his return for all of his own. J. A. T. Robinson contests the view (pp. 325–29).

13. John 3:14–15. Snake of Brass & Son of Man

	Jewish Scriptures (Num 21:4–9)	Fourth Gospel
Comparison	Just as . . .	So
Agent(s)	Moses (on God's instructions)	[God ("divine passive") & humans]
Action	Raised	Lifted up (exaltation/crucifixion?)
Object	Serpent: unclean animal (Lev 11:42–44)	Son of Man
Material	Image making forbidden (2nd command)	[Image of God in humans]

1. At the outset, we have to ask ourselves, "What is wrong with the OT picture!"?

2. Chapman (187–91) is unique in developing the analogy fully, most commentators saying that the lifting up is the only significant point of comparison.

3. Consider these dislocating/disorienting features of the original account:

   a. Fashioning the object violated the Second Commandment (Exod 20:4//Deut 5:8).

   b. That Moses himself formed it aggravates the deed.

   c. That God ordered him to do so makes matters worse.

   d. Were not snakes, according to kosher Law (Lev 11:42–44), to be regarded as unclean (not to mention, dangerous!)?

   e. How did the cause of the problem become its solution? That it continued being problematic (though in a different way) is pointed out by Chapman (189): during his reform of Judah's idolatrous practices, King Hezekiah shattered the brass snake that Moses had made because, for many centuries since, the people had been offering incense to the image in worship (2 Kings 18:1–4).

4. Is there anything in the story of Jesus (even at this early stage in the narrative) that would identify him as threatening to Israel's institutions and destructive of its Law? What of John's fuller account?

5. On analogy, how might the Son of Man/Jesus, the cause of the Jews' problem, be their solution/salvation?

6. In addition to its being an ironic reference to Jesus' death/exaltation on the cross, the son of man's lifting up might also allude to the son of man figure of Dan 7:13–14 who is [to be] exalted by the Ancient of Days with a kingdom that he did not previously possess, elevated to an authority that he had not earlier exercised, and granted glory that he had not heretofore "enjoyed." See also FP 17, n. 8.

14. John 3:16. As if for the First Time (and in Context)

Categories	John 3:16	Johannine Context
1. Who? (subject)	God (source)	Revealer
2. What? #1 (action)	Loved	Self-Disclosure (5:20)
3. Whom? #1 (object)	The world	The inhabited earth, not a portion of it
4. What? #2 (action)	Gave	= "Sent"
5. Whom? #2 (object)	Son (agent)	Reveal the Father (1:18, 17:6, 8, 14); to do Father's will (5:19–30)
6. How? (means)	Is believing	Relying on Jesus: God's best revelation
7. So what? (-result)	Not perish	The opposite of #8
8. So what? (+result)	Eternal (aeonic) life	Knowing the true God & Jesus Christ (17:3)

1. Does this "Golden Verse," as it stands, say anything about Jesus' being sent to die on the cross for the world's sins?

2. When this single text is read in context, rather than harmonized with other statements in the NT (or filtered through a Pauline lens or that of a particular confessional theology), several fresh readings are both possible and probable.

3. Is "everlasting life" (quantity) the goal—the never-ending persistence of the ego? The translation "eternal life" is more indebted to the Latin

rendering of the Greek—which more likely refers to "the life of the age/aeon" [to come]—a matter of quality.

4.   Note the key definition for eternal/aeonian life, supplied by Jesus himself, at 17:3. (Keep in mind the cluster of terms for revelation (FP 4): "knowledge," "light," "truth," "teaching," "witness," etc.) Some interpreters take this to mean that knowing God and Jesus is the basis for eventual eternal life. However, the statement indicates that such (relational) knowledge is the very life itself. That it is a present reality (as well as a future one) corresponds to the continuous action of the verbs for "believing" and "having." (The noun "faith"/"belief" never occurs. Stasis is not an option.)

5.   Believing should be understood more in the sense of "relying" or "trusting" (again, continuous action, not once-for-all, according to the Greek)—that Jesus is the best revelation of God (rather than other sources, written or otherwise).

6.   What difference might such an interpretation make to the nature and conduct of evangelism and Christian formation?

15. Father & Son: Mutual Knowledge in John & the Synoptics

	Matt 11:27	Luke 10:22	John 3:35	John 10:15	John 13:3	John 17:1–2	John 17:25
1	All things	All things	All things		All things	All authority	
2	Handed over	Handed over	Placed in		Had given	Have given	
3	Me by	Me by	Son's hands		His hands	Him (Son, v. 1)	
4	My Father	My Father	Father		Father	Father (v. 1)	
5	None knows	None knows		Knows	Knowing		
6	Son	Son		Son	Jesus		
7	Except Father	Except Father		Father			

	Matt 11:27	Luke 10:22	John 3:35	John 10:15	John 13:3	John 17:1–2	John 17:25
8	None knows	[None knows]					
9	Father	Father		Father			Father
10	Except Son	Except Son		I know			I know
11	Anyone	Anyone					
12	Son	Son					I
13	Reveals	Reveals					Have made known
	Him	Him					

1. Many scholars, seeing such close correspondence between Matthew and Luke, posit a common source (whether oral or written) that they label "Q"—which each Evangelist adopted, adapted, and arranged according to literary-theological aims. "Q" comes from the German "Quelle" (source).

2. This is yet another striking example of how prominent the general theme of revelation is in the FG, the vocabulary of "knowing" being especially prevalent when intimate, interpersonal relations are being described. It helps to define the nature of friendship—friends being people "in the know" (15:15). Self-giving love and obedience are intimately bound up with such knowledge (vv. 13–14). Such mutuality has been foundational to Charles Williams' model of interpersonal sharing, which he termed "co-inherence" (p. 92).

3. Is it any wonder that scholars have cited with approval the description of this atypical dynamic in the SG as "a thunderbolt from the Johannine sky?" The statement was originally made by Karl von Hase (p. 422). Others see this as evidence that the transmitters of both gospel traditions have adapted earlier, less-formulated oral material in keeping with the desire to meet the needs of their readers.

16. John 5:17–30. Subordinationist Sonship/ Christology (See 1:18)

	Father	Son
1	My Father is working still (17);	and also I am working.
2	The Son is unable to do a single thing from himself unless he sees the Father doing (it);	
3	for whatever he does (19c)	the Son does likewise.
4	For the Father loves the Son (20)	
5	and shows him all that he is doing.	
6	and greater things will he show him.	
7	For just as the Father raises the dead (21)	
8	and gives life	so also the Son
9		makes alive whomever he wishes.
10	For the Father judges no one; (22)	
11	but he has given all judgment	to the Son.
12	For just as the Father has life in himself, (26)	
13	so also he has given	to the Son to have life in himself.
14	And he has given him authority	
15	to make judgment (27)	because he is a son of man.
16	I am unable to do a single thing by myself; as I hear, I judge. And my judgment is just	
17	because I am not seeking to do my own will but the will of the one who sent me (30)	

1. Could you make a case that this passage is a microcosm of the FG?

2. Might one view this as an elaboration/particularization of 1:18? The Greek behind "has made him known" could woodenly be translated, "has exegeted him"/"has led him out." The Latin has *enarravit*: again, woodenly, "has narrated him"/"has told his story."

3. Is it somewhat ironic, when appealing to the FG for proofs of the "highest" Christology, that one finds Jesus himself being profoundly theo-/patri-centric?

4. Does one usually think of Jesus' authority and ability to have been both derivative and dependent, respectively? It should not come as a surprise for those who have been attentive to God's relation with Israel—God's firstborn son (Exod 4:22).

5. As the delegated and designated Son, Jesus has been qualified to be the Father's ambassador extraordinaire and plenipotentiary. He is therefore authorized to speak and act (only) on behalf of the one who sent him. He is the ultimate Apostle (*apostellein*). To hear and to see the Son is to hear and see the Father—not because Jesus and the Father are one and the same person but because he can be believed/relied upon to carry out this role (negatively, not to be a renegade son—as Israel often was).

6. Thus, to dishonor the Son is to dishonor the Father (v. 23).

7. Sonship is always "bipolar": status/identity must be complemented by role/task/assignment. This requires attitude and action, believing and behaving, trusting and obeying.

8. Traditional Christian theology has distinguished between the states of the pre-incarnate and incarnate Second Person of the Trinity. The limitations imposed upon or freely taken upon the latter are not characteristic of the former. It is because of this distinction that Jesus can say, "The Father is greater than I" (14:28). Although Jesus is the way, the truth, and the life, the destination is the Father (14:6).

17. John 6:40–68. Consuming the Son of Man's Flesh & Blood

vv.	(1)	(2)	(3)	(4)	(5)	(6)
40	SEEing & BELIEVing			In the SON, HIM	having LIFE	of the Age
47	BELIEVing				having LIFE	of the Age
51		EATS	bread		will LIVE	into the Age
			bread=my FLESH		LIFE	for world
53		unless EAT & drink	FLESH & blood SM		no LIFE	
54		CHEWing & drinking	my FLESH & blood		having LIFE	of the Age
55			my FLESH=true food / my blood=true drink			
56		CHEWing & drink	my FLESH & my blood	mutual ABIDing		
57		CHEWing	me		will LIVE	
58		CHEWing	bread		will LIVE	into the Age
63			[one's] FLESH	SPIRIT	is giving LIFE	
					useless	
			my WORDS	SPIRIT	LIFE	
68–69	BELIEVED & COME TO KNOW		WORDS	of the SON of GOD	LIFE	of the Age

1. I have stressed the present continuous action of the Greek verbs in columns 1, 2, and 5 because they are rarely expressed in English translations. This underscores the fact that the author does not focus on a single, individual act done in the past or of a purely future state/era.

2. In vv. 54–58, the more general language of "eating" in vv. 51 and 53 gives way in the Greek to the more graphic language of "chewing/masticating/gnawing"—again, rarely reflected in translations.

3. So far as numbers are concerned, the terminology of consumption outweighs that of believ(ing). And yet the eating/chewing of the Son of Man (53) is "sandwiched" or bounded by trusting/relying on the Son (of God) in vv. 40 and 68.

4. Similarly, the vocabulary of "flesh" (vv. 51–56) converges with that of "believing," of "words" and "spirit" (along with the denial in v. 63 [cols. 3, 5] that "flesh" other than Jesus' has any effect).

5. Whatever the means, the outcome is identical: "life of the age [to come]," routinely rendered by the misleading "eternal [=everlasting] life."

6. The mutual "abiding" of v. 56 suggests a link to 15:4–10 and a hint that, in addition to this passage, other texts speak of relating to Jesus according to alternative imagery. For these, see FP 31.

7. How might such observations affect one's view of the Eucharist?

8. That Jesus speaks of consuming the *son of man's* flesh (not the son of God's, nor the Messiah's) and the vulnerability that it suggests could be a reflection of the expression's being (at base) an idiom for the downside of human experience: its at-riskness and vulnerability—as argued for by Bowker as well as Lemcio (2005).

18. Jesus & Asclepios: Healers Extraordinaire

	Jesus	Asclepios
1. What? (event)	Cure of illnesses	Cure of illnesses
2. Conditions	None/once: faith (in God)	Some (pre- or post-)
3. Response(s)	Nothing tangible	Presents, inscriptions
4. To Whom? (object)	Praise to God	Praise to Asclepios
5. Where? (place)	Anywhere	Temple of Asclepios
6. When? (time)	Anytime (except at night)	At night
7. (Occasion)	Publicly	Privately, during dream
8. (Ideology)	Signs of eternal/aonian life	(Universal good)

1. Perhaps the most widely known healer in the ancient world was the alleged divine man Asclepios. His activity is sometimes put forward by scholars as a model from which the Gospel writers drew when portraying the role of Jesus as healer. However, such claims must be evaluated in terms of closer analysis, which the FP above helps to conduct. These data hold true for healings in the other Gospels too. See C & D pp. 151–52 for the texts, which I have selected because these inscriptions clearly predate the Gospels. Kee (pp. 144–46) provides a somewhat expanded collection of the material, with variations in translation that, however, do not affect the point being made here. Dittenberger's critical edition of the originals remains standard.

2. As always, the dating of such parallels must be attended to: as contemporary or earlier than the Gospel accounts. This is where the instances collected by C & D (even in the latest edition of 1994) must be examined carefully. Few of their samples come with dates (even approximate ones). One has to rule out the possibility that some examples from the Greco-Roman world might have been influenced by Gospel accounts.

3. A. E. Harvey (pp. 115–17) has observed that, among healing accounts throughout the ancient world, it is Jesus who is reported in the Gospels to have performed the most cures among the paralyzed, blind, deaf, and mute. In the Jewish world, no one has been reported as doing so. Thus, among his contemporaries, he was unique in this regard as well. Furthermore, these four constitute most of the healings within the Gospels themselves. In the light of Isaiah 35:5–6, what might Jesus or the Evangelist be implying by such a concentration of these particular miracles ("signs" in the FG)—especially if they represented congenital conditions, in some instances, at least (as in the case of the man blind from birth in John 9)?

4. While Jesus accepts the occasional expression of faith that he or God can perform the cure (categories 2 and 3), he never requires it as a precondition. What does this phenomenon imply, so far as the concept of grace is concerned?

5. Although Jesus is certainly the agent of such demonstrations of power, their source is always God, who is also the subject of praise given by the astonished onlookers. What is the case with Asclepios?

6. In the SG, Jesus occasionally cures in private (#5)—the situation either dictating it (among the tombs, Mark 5:1–20) or because he deliberately withdraws with the petitioner (7:31–37, 8:22–26). All of the instances in John (because they are signs?) are public.

7. While the differences in most of the categories above are obvious, discerning ideology (#8) has to be more subtle.

19. John 10:30 (& 17:11, 21–23). "I and the Father Are One"

10:30	17:11a	17:11b	17:21a	17:21b	17:21c		17:22a	17:22b	17:23
I and	may	as	May	as	I	they	they	I in them	they
Father are	Father: they be	we are	they all be	you Father in me	in you	in us	may be	you in me	may be
one (*hen*)	one (*hen*)	one (*hen*)	one (*hen*)				one (*hen*)		one (*hen*)
									perfectly

38

1. Two extremes are to be avoided (especially when interpreting the FG): claiming too much about Jesus—and to little. This is one of those instances where apologists may rush in to find grist for theological mills where none exists.

2. All too often, John 10:30 is not read in relation to 17:11 and 21–23, where comparisons are drawn regarding the nature of the unity being urged among the disciples. Is it about nature in this case? What other kind of unity may be predicated of Jesus and God that would match that which should exist between his followers and them?

3. The form of the Greek for "one" at this point is *hen* (the neuter singular) rather than *heis* (the masculine singular). Had John used the latter, he would have made Jesus claim *identity* with the Father rather than unity with him.

20. John 10:30–38; 5:17–30. Restrained Christology in John & the Synoptics

Pattern	John 5:17–30	John 10:30–38	Mark (1–8, esp. 8:27–33)
1. Public claim	Father & Son at work	I & Father are one	SM: authority, lord
2. Public reaction	Make self God's equal	Make yourself God	You are the Messiah!
3. Backing off	I can do nothing of myself	Ps 82: you are gods	Tell no one
4. Citing behavior	See & hear → do & say	Son sent into world	SM must s-d-r
	Father-Son apprenticeship	Does Father's works	

(s = suffer, d = die, r = be raised)

40

1. Mark's Gospel is laced with Jesus' attempts to prevent quasi-titles from being applied to him. This has given rise to the so-called "messianic" or "son of God" secrecy theory made in/famous by William Wrede. John (it is often said by scholars) will have nothing to do with it.

2. Nevertheless, if one shifts to the more accurate categories of privacy for the SG and restraint for the FG, then the gulf between them may not be so vast (or seem so fixed).

3. The result is that in the two most explicit places in the FG where Jesus (1) makes public statements about his relation to God, there is (3) almost an immediate backing off when the point is (2) pressed by the audience.

4. As it seems more than coincidental, perhaps the phenomenon had been deeply embedded in the minds of the disciples who had first heard the statements or in the consciousness of those who had transmitted each tradition—first orally and then in writing.

5. Many Christians have been schooled to believe that Jesus everywhere proclaimed himself to be the Messiah/Son of God—or at least allowed others to do so. However, the evidence from the SG does not allow this view (see Lemcio 2012, pp. 58–60.); neither is it the case within the FG if one keeps coming back to these responses of Jesus.

6. The sort of demurral seen in both Gospel traditions might be understood in the following manner. The Synoptic Jesus says, in effect, "Do not speak of me as Son/Messiah *until* the Son of Man is raised from the dead," as in Mark 9:9. The Johannine Jesus says, "Do not regard me as Son *without* acknowledging my dependence upon the Father for all that I say and do" (as in these chapters). The former is a diachronic emphasis (a linear portrait through time); the latter is a synchronic one (a slice-of-life-at-any-point kind of portrayal).

21. John 11:1–46 & Luke 10:38–42.
A Tale of Two Sisters

	Mary	Martha
Luke 10:38–42	Affirmed as a learner	Chided
John 11:1–46	Subordinated to sister	Theologically astute

1. Do we have here a common tradition taken in two directions by each evangelist?

2. Both sisters are active in John 11. But who is the more so? What evidence do you cite?

3. If the author of the FG has Luke in mind, does he want his audience to infer that Martha had gotten the point by the time that John wrote? Or, are we faced with two different traditions about the two sisters?

4. It is apparent that these Jewish women have no problem at all in addressing a male, a rabbi (their friend). Martha seems even to take a scolding tone to Jesus (11:32). Does she remind you of the feisty Samaritan woman in ch. 4, who is herself portrayed as no mean theologian and evangelist—unlike that of Nicodemus ("*the* [not "a"] Teacher of Israel" in ch. 3)?

5. That such interaction between the sexes was more widespread than realized is also evidenced by the group of mourners "of the Jews" who had arrived to comfort the bereft sisters (vv. 33–37). This should help put to rest the common, unfounded assertions that such easy interaction did not occur among the Jews of Jesus' day—an attitude that he alone came to dispel. See the important corrective provided by Amy-Jill Levine (pp. 131–38 and the literature cited there).

6. For a study of four other women in the FG who act as agents of revelation (or explication), see Dorothy Lee (brought to my attention by Maloney).

22. Lazarus & Jesus

	Lazarus (ch. 11)	Jesus (throughout)
1. What? #1 (action)	Resuscitation	Resurrection
2. From whom? (source)	God/Father (41)	God (10:18)
3. By Whom? (agent)	Jesus (42)	Jesus (2:19–21, 10:17–18)
4. How? (manner)	By spoken word	By divine action
5. Where? (place)	Tomb in Bethany (38)	Tomb in Jerusalem (20:1)
6. How Long? (duration)	Four days (17, 39)	Three days (2:19–21)
7. Clothing	Facecloth (44)	Facecloth (20:7)
8. What? #2 (Jews' reaction)	Kill him (12:9–11)	Kill him (11:50–53)
9. Why? (reason)	Many believe in Jesus (11)	One die for nation (11:50–52)

1. The Lazarus story is commonly viewed as a foreshadowing of subsequent events regarding Jesus. Despite the obvious "parallels," what are the clear distinctions between the two?

2. Although the same word in Greek is used to speak of Lazarus' "rising up" as in the case of Jesus, what is the difference between the two experiences of returning to life (11:23–24 and 20:17)?

3. All of the Gospels (and the NT as a whole) make a clear distinction between God as the source of divine action and Jesus as its agent (11:41–42). Unique in all of the NT is Jesus' claim (#3) that he is the agent of his own resurrection (otherwise, it is always said that God raised Jesus from the dead). However, from whom does such authority derive, according to 2:18?

43

23. John 12:31–33 & Mark 3:27. World Ruler Expelled & Strong Man (Satan) Bound

	World Ruler (John 12:31–33)	Strong Man (Mark 3:27)
1. Who? (object)	Satan/Caesar	Satan
2. What? (act)	Expulsion	Binding
3. By whom? (agent)	Divine passive (=God)	Stronger man (Jesus)
4. When? (time)	Near future: "now"	Recent past
5. Where? (place/occasion)	At the cross	At the temptation (1:13)

1. According to the Markan account, a decisive action against the devil had been taken at the desert testing (the only prior event where Satan is mentioned, according to the analogy drawn).

2. Who are the candidates for "the ruler of this world"? Does one have to be precise? Might John have been deliberately vague—not only with regard to a supernatural or human one but also with regard to a particular human ruler? More than one of the latter might fit the bill—depending upon the circumstances of the reader (across time and culture).

3. At what point in human history do Christians usually assign the binding or expulsion of the world ruler, if he is to be identified as Satan/the devil? Whether during his life or at the moment of his death, Jesus dealt dramatically with the powers that be.

4. Regarding the act of expulsion: might the context be a legal one—where the judge ejects the prosecuting attorney/adversarial counsel

(*Satan* in Hebrew means "adversary.") for contempt of court? George Caird has suggested this forensic image when he interprets Michael's expulsion of Satan/the Devil/Dragon/Serpent from the heavenly realms in Revelation 12:7–10. Might the two Johns be referring to the same event using different modes of expression?

5. According to 16:11, the one who has been cast out has also been judged.

24. John 12:37–48 & Isaiah 6:9–10.
The Reason for Performing Signs

(Matt 13:1–23//Mark 4:1–20//Luke 8:4–18)

	Resistance	Consequence (1)	Consequence (2)
Isaiah	Rebellious Children (chs. 1–5)	Blindness/deafness (6:9–10)	No turning, healing but destruction (6:11–13)
	(Israel: elect, saved)		
John	Hostility to Jesus (chs. 2–11)	Blindness & hardness (12:40)	Could not believe, be healed (12:39–40)
	(By religious leaders of Jews)		The crowd (12:34)

46

1. It is no wonder that Christian preachers, appealing for commitments to mission of one sort or another after reading the call of Isaiah, stop short after v. 8: "Then said I, 'Here am I; send me'!" What follows does not constitute an enviable assignment.

2. Apart from this, commentators go to extraordinary lengths to explain (away) the harshness of Jesus' (or the Evangelist's) replies that the purpose of his parables and signs (according to Mark 4:10–12) was to blind and deafen and to harden hearts, thereby effectively cutting off the possibility of repentance. So, one reads that the underlying Aramaic was mistranslated, or that the Gospel writers' harsher theology needs to be distinguished from the historical Jesus' actual teaching, etc. However, if Mark 4 and John 12 are read in the context of Isaiah 1–3 and 2–11 (respectively), and Isaiah 6 is read in the context of chapters 1–5, then such drastic, desperate, and artificial moves are not needed. In both instances, the history of rebellion by God's people reaches a point of no return such that the prophetic word and enacted sign, which would otherwise have stimulated spiritual sensitivity, become the cause of hardened sensibilities—with its disastrous results.

25. John 12:37–40 & Isaiah 1–6.
Prophecy in Context

(Matt 13:1–23//Mark 4:1–20//Luke 8:4–18)

	Isaiah 1–5, 6	John 2–11, 12:37–40
1. Who? (subject/source)	God	God
2. What? (event)	Judgment	Judgment
3. Against whom? (object)	People of Judah	The people
4. Why? (reason/cause)	Rebellion (chs. 1–5)	Opposition to Jesus (chs. 1–11)
5. By whom? (agent)	Isaiah (ch. 6)	Jesus (ch. 12)
6. How? (means)	Proclamation (6:9–10)	Signs, words (12:37, 48–50)
7. Result: deliberate (1)	Spiritual insensitivity	Spiritual insensitivity
	No turning or healing	No repentance/healing
8. Result: deliberate (2)	Cities destroyed, fields burned	Judgment on the Last Day (12:48)
9. So what? (significance)	Opportunity runs out	Opportunity runs out
10. When? (time)	Several centuries BCE	First century CE
11. Where? (place)	Judah	Temple in Jerusalem

1. This display shows even more graphically than in FP 24 how John appears to make parallel the situation in Isaiah's day—several centuries before—and Jesus' own experience.

2. It should also prevent the use of these passages as prooftexts for individual determinism. The context clearly speaks about the destiny of a community and of a people (God's own people!)—something that the Isaiah passage makes especially clear.

3. What is the difference between the time and quality of resulting judgment (#7)?

26. John 12:44. In Whom Does One Believe?
A Bridge Too Far (2)?

	John 12:44	Mark 9:37
1. Responder	The one who is	The one who is
2. Response	believing in	receiving
3. *Jesus*	me	me
4. Denial	does not	does not
5. Response	believe	receive
6. *Jesus*	in me	me
7. Contrast	but	but
6. God	in the one	the one
	who sent	who sent
7. *Jesus*	me	me

1. It might come as a shock to the reader that, after eleven chapters of calling for belief in himself, Jesus makes this public outcry—in the Jerusalem temple!

2. Even though not a single manuscript exists with the word "only," the NIV translators inserted it after the second "in me." Many years ago, as a seminary student, I pressed a visiting member of the "Panel of Fifteen" who had overseen the project on why this was so. He responded candidly that they wanted to ensure that there would not appear to be a contradiction between this and Jesus' earlier expressions. (This was consistent with the project's commitment to the inerrancy of Scripture.) Somewhat brashly, I suggested to him that such apologetics did not belong in the translator's portfolio.

3. Ironically, this addition worked against the translators' "philosophy": it resulted in disassembling one of the few bridges that occurs between the Johannine and Synoptic traditions.

49

4. Such a theo-/patricentric emphasis had been anticipated earlier at
    5:24: "The one who goes on hearing my word and continually be-
    lieves him who sent me is having eternal/aeonian life."

5. It is well to remember E. C. Hoskyns' dramatic dictum: "Chris-
    tian faith is not a cult of Jesus; it is faith in God (xiii. 20; Matt. x.
    40; Luke ix. 48; I Thess. i. 9)." Both are eligible subjects of faith
    because of their mutual indwelling (p. 430) and because, in word
    and deed, the Son speaks and performs only that which the Father
    says and does (FP 16).

27. John 13:1–17. Lord & Teacher.
Servant Son of Man (the Synoptics)

	John 13:1–17	Mark 10:42–45	Luke 22:21–27
Setting	(Passover) dinner	Status debate	Passover dinner
Who? (Christology)	Teacher & Lord (13, 14)	The Son of Man	The Son of Man
What? (act)	Washing disciples' feet	Service = Release	Serving at table
Where? (place)	Jerusalem	Way to Jerusalem	Jerusalem
When? (time)	Final week	?	Final week

1. Here is another instance (see FP 8) where the language of teaching appears (to us) in unusual company—twice.

2. What have lords done historically? What have teachers often done? How are these roles, so often expressive of conventional notions of power and leadership, subverted and redefined? St. Paul's version of this reversal may be found in Philippians 2:1–11.

3. At least since the Middle Ages, popes of the Roman Catholic Church have regularly applied to themselves the title *Servus Servorum Dei* ("Servant of the Servants of God").

28. John 13:34–35, 15:12–13.
The Love Command in Leviticus, Matthew, & John

	(A)	(B)	(C)
Who? (subjects)	Leviticus	Matthew	John 13:34–35, 15:12–13
1. Love neighbor			Love one another
—Fellow Israelite			—As I have loved you
—As self	(19:18)	(22:39)	
2. Love stranger			
—As self	(19:34)		
3. Love enemies		(5:43–48)	[God so loved the world (3:16)]
—Pray for them			
—Do them good		[Also Luke 6:27]	

1. John is routinely regarded as a "sectarian"—chiefly because Jesus' teaching about loving is confined to the disciples. From an ecclesiastical point of view, this term has been applied to groups who refuse to be subordinate to the dominant religious authority. (In that sense, from the view of first-century Jews, the entire Christian movement could have been regarded as such, not just its Johannine stream.) It is not simply a synonym for an alienated, marginal, or exclusive body. A refreshing (rare) attention to the range of uses and nuances is provided by Kåre Sigvald Fuglseth.

2. Consider the following pastoral dimensions:

   a. The community of disciples for which Jesus prays was apparently fragmented or in danger of becoming so. Otherwise, why pray for unity (even *perfect* unity) three times (17:11, 21–23)?

   b. So, would it not be a cruel irony to invite an outsider into a community where insiders could not get along? Would it not be vital first to "get their act together"?

3. In what sense is Jesus' teaching a "new" commandment (C), especially in light of the commands in Leviticus (A)—which (though routinely ignored) include loving the stranger/alien/non-Israelite/the "other" as oneself?

29. John 14 & 16.
The *Parakletos*: What's in a Name?

Versions	Translation	(Perceived) Meaning
1. AV	Comforter	More interpersonal
2. ASV		
3. CEB	Companion (fn. Advocate)	More interpersonal
4. JB		
5. NEB	Advocate	Forensic/juridical
6. NIV	Counselor	Forensic/juridical, therapeutic (the spirit of the age)
7. NRSV	Advocate (fn Helper)	Forensic/juridical
8. OSB	Helper	General assistance?
9. RSV	Counselor	General assistance?

1. Literally, this term means "called alongside."

2. "Comforter," "Companion," and "Helper" tend to be regarded as informal, individualistic, and interpersonal.

3. "Counselor," given the temperament of the current age, is liable to be interpreted in therapeutic terms, once again suggesting an individualistic, though more formal role. Yet, the forensic/legal is not far away—as in "counsel for the defense."

4. Although "Advocate" might be viewed as more general and interpersonal (and individualistic), it can also convey a more juridical sense.

5. Both "Advocate" and "Counselor" would be fitting in the sense of a defense attorney if it could be shown that Satan in the FG functions as the prosecuting attorney (or adversarial counsel). After all, *Satan* in Hebrew means "adversary" or "accuser."

6. Thus, one could take "comfort" in having such a figure stand beside one in court.

7. A clearer, more collective understanding occurs outside of the FG, as in "Who shall lay charge [*engkalein*] against God's elect?" (Rom 8:33) or "The accuser [*katēgōr*] of our brothers and sisters who accuses [*katēgorein*] them day and night" (Rev 12:10). Here, God's people as

a community seem to be the defendants.

8. This counselor's more aggressive role comes to the fore in 16:8–11, where the Holy Spirit functions almost as a prosecuting attorney! According to v. 11, "the ruler of this world," having been cast out (12:31), has also been judged (see FP 23).

9. Jesus also refers to this figure as "the Spirit of truth" (14:17, 16:13), which fits with the revelatory emphasis of the FG. The legal expert (who is also full of integrity) knows more than his defendant, and he has the skills to put such knowledge into practice.

10. In addition to spirit, truth is also vital to the worship of the Father (4:23–24).

30. Their Day in Court: Satan & the Holy Spirit

	Satan/Devil	Holy Spirit
Role (1)	Adversarial counsel	Defense counsel (*parakletos*)
	Prosecuting attorney	Defense attorney
Revelation: +/-	Liar, father of lies (8:44)	"Spirit of truth" (14:17, 15:26, 16:13)
Outcome	Murderer from the beginning	Spirit gives life (6:63)
Role (2)	Condemned/judged (16:11)	Spirit as aggressor (16:7–11)

1. One needs to resist the temptation of reading into particular texts, notions drawn from other texts and popular culture—both within and outside of the church. If we take seriously the meaning of the Hebrew *satan*, as "adversary," and the Greek *parakletos*, as "advocate" (or "counselor," in the legal—not therapeutic—sense), then the image of a courtroom drama fits the specific vocabulary and dynamics of the FG.

2. Since "truth" belongs to the cluster of revelatory terms (FP 4), and that one of the appellations for the Spirit is "the Spirit of truth," then the theme becomes even more apparent.

3. Getting at the truth should be the goal of all concerned; however, distortion, obfuscation, suppression of evidence, abuse of witnesses, etc. could work in the interests of either plaintiff or defendant. It is in this context that Jesus' naming of Satan as "father of lies" takes on special meaning (8:44). Should one be surprised that opposing him would take the form of waging a war of words by the Incarnate Word?

4. How does the accusation of "murderer" relate to that of "father of lies?" Are there circumstances where desperate parties would resort to anything to keep the truth from coming to *light*—another revelatory term? Does not darkness (anti-revelation) serve to cover up evil (see also 3:19–2)?5. Throughout the course of the case, evidence

(signs) pro and con is presented. The testimony of witnesses (two more revelatory expressions) is evaluated. They are cross-examined, for none is infallible in what s/he sees and hears.

5.   When Jesus describes/assigns another role to the Holy Spirit in 16:7–11, is he still functioning as *defense* attorney?

6.   Do these passages provide the context for Jesus' statement in 12:31 that "the ruler of this world [whether the devil or Caesar] will now be cast out" (i.e., at the moment of Jesus' death, v. 33)? Already judged (according to 16:11), will he also suffer the ignominy of being thrown out *of court* for contempt?

31. Relating to the Father Through the Son: Six Images

Image	3. Generative	4. Aquatic	6. Cultic	10. Pastoral	15. Horticultural	17. Communal
1. Christology	Teacher	Well	"Victim"	Shepherd	Branch	Priest
2. Response(s)	Be born from above of water, believe	Drink water	Eat body Drink blood	Follow, hear voice (3–16)	Abide in the branch, be pruned (4–7)	Be one
3.		Never thirst (14)	Never thirst (35)			
4.		Food = do will of God (34)	Food → eternal life (27)			
5.		Abide (40)	Abide (27, 56)		Abide	
6.			Word			Word
7.	& of spirit (5–6)	God is Spirit Spirit & truth (24)	Spirit gives life			
8.	Know these things (10–11)	know (*oida*): the Savior of the world (42)	come to know	know (14–15)	know	know

57

1. Perhaps most, if not all, readers of the FG are inclined to think that believing in Jesus (always a verb, never a noun, and mostly in the continuous action) is the primary if not exclusive means of relating to Jesus. And yet, might this mode be(come) too mental and passive?

2. However, the FP above indicates that there are several other means by which to "connect" with the risen Jesus, none of which seems to have been given priority. Is there at least a red flag raised as a warning about choosing the image closest to one's upbringing—rationalist, cultic, behavioral, etc.? In a similar vein, Gail O'Day observes,

   > It is the Fourth Evangelist's freedom in making use of such a "total register" ["of images, metaphors, and stories," citing Wilder, p. 92] that gives the Fourth Gospel its richness and power. The Fourth Gospel's narrative makes available to the reader an experience of Jesus and the God known in Jesus in ways that resist our attempts to assimilate them into systematic categories. (p. 113)

3. And they are different enough to caution the reader about harmonizing them. Such diversity also ought to prevent reducing all to a single principle or essence. Stated another way, since none tells the entire (or even the most important) story, no single image/metaphor and its supporting dialect or idiom should be elevated above or isolated from the others.

4. To illustrate, consider the image of a gem (or even cut glass), which is made of *multiple* **facets**.

5. While two-dimensional plate glass is desired for seeing directly through a window, lovers prefer the *many*-**sidedness** of a jewel. It is the *various* **angles** of vision that give the object such great worth. Every turn of the gem enables another aspect of the whole to be glimpsed. *No one* **surface** enjoys the priority.

6. Furthermore, the full reality of a diamond is greater than the sum of all of its **facets**. Likewise, Reality cannot be confined nor exhausted by these images, experiences, and expressions of it.

7. Just as the object retains a single reality even as the admirer examines its *different* **planes**, so the Reality for which it stands remains stable during *various* times, places, circumstances, and beholders.

8. Just as carbon is common to each aspect of "diamondness," so knowledge is common to each of the metaphors in the FG.

32. John 19:28, 30. "It [What?] Is Finished!"

	Sinai Covenant (Exod 24:1–8)	Day of Atonement (Leviticus 16)	Passover (Exodus 12)	Jesus' death (John 19)
Sacrificial victim	Ox(en)	2 Goats —slain —freed ("scapegoat")	Lamb(s)	Jesus
Purpose/result	Sealing/bonding of the **community**	Release from the **community's** sins by the **live** animal	Protection → liberation of the **community** from Egyptian slavery	Protection
Date/time	No annual observance	Late summer or early fall	Spring	Day of Preparation (31, 42)

1. The blood sacrifices of three different animals achieved different results at different times of the year.

2. Sacrifices were for those who were *already* God's people, called by him into special relationship as early as Genesis 12:1–3. They were not initiatory rites.

3. The Passover sacrifice (Exod 12) was not for the forgiveness of sins, nor was covenant bonding (Exod 24:1–8). The former celebrated the **community's** freedom from Egypt so that Israel as a **people** could be joined by covenant to God (the latter).

4. Sacrifices on the Day of Atonement did not *get* Israelites "saved"; they *kept* them "saved"—salvation not understood as going to heaven and avoiding hell.

5. Jesus did not die on the Day of Atonement (which was almost six months apart from Passover).

6. Define the significance of Jesus' death contextually, keeping in mind the earlier discussion of John 1:49.

7. More closely, examine John 17:4, where Jesus uses the same verb for finishing or completing in his so-called High Priestly Prayer. His statements in the immediate context concur with the dominant theme of the FG—17:6, 8, 14, 26. Is anything said about forgiveness of sins? But, given the classic significance of Passover, does the *word* of Jesus protect his own from the Evil One?

8. Note that protection is the point of Jesus' laying down his life for his sheep—between them and the attacking animal (10:11–15).

9. What was Jesus' death to achieve, according to 12:31–33 (see FP 23)? Think about all of these statements (FP 33) as facets of a gem: a reality too large to be encompassed by a single image—or doctrine.

10. The challenge is to not impose another's view about the significance of the cross upon the FG—whether that be St. Paul's or a systematic theologian's articulating a particular confessional commitment.

33. The Death of Jesus

Effect	Scriptural Backgrounds	John
1. Sin-bearing	Removal (Day of Atonement): Israel's sins (Lev 16:20–22)	Removal (Days of Atonement): the world's sin (1:29)
2. Offering	Protection (Passover) by substitution (Exod 12)	Protection of "sheep" by interposition (10:11–5)
3. Nation saved		One instead of all (11:50–53)
4. Multiplication		Dying single grain → much fruit (12:24)
5. Glorification		Father's name glorified (12:27–28)
6. Attraction		Lifting up: all people drawn (12:32–33)
7. Judgment		The world's judgment (12:31)
8. Expulsion		World ruler cast out
9. Offering	Protection (Passover) by substitution (Exod 12)	Day of Preparation (19:14, 30–31)

The numbers that follow are keyed to those in the FP:

1. As we saw earlier in FP 7, the grammar of 1:29 shows Jesus as continually taking away the sin [not sins] of the world during his life. This declaration by John the Baptizer establishes the theme very early on. Is any blood being shed in this process? Was the "scapegoat" killed on the Day of Atonement?

2. Whereas blood was shed at Passover, does death necessarily occur in the interposition of the shepherd between the attacking animal and the sheep? Can he protect them if he is dead?

3. The ironic prophecy of Caiaphas certainly expects death.

4. Although death is fundamental to the grain analogy, is blood involved here?

5. Who is to be glorified by Jesus' death? What does this mean? Relate to the main theme the aspects of glory as weight and brilliance.

6. The lifting up is ironic: exaltation to a throne or to a cross (or with exaltation and cross being redefined, in either case). Certainly, the spilling of blood would occur here.

7. In # 5–8, death by crucifixion is certainly in view.

8. Recall that Passover brought about the protection of the Israelite households from the destroying angel, whose assignment was to strike the firstborn male of every household, Israelite and Egyptian.

9. What can be said about the significance that John sees in Jesus' death? Is it limited to a single, preferred image? Does one absorb/harmonize the others? Can the variety be reduced to a principle? Is blood fundamental?

10. Is it significant that, for # 3–8, there is no OT "background"? Does it mean that enhancement is at least as significant as fulfillment? Apply what you learned in FP 31 to this multi-dimensional character of Jesus' death—and to the promise of Jesus that that Spirit would lead his disciples to all of the truth (16:13).

11. What is the significance of the fact that the vocabulary of forgiveness is entirely absent prior to the resurrection—that it is not associated with Jesus' death? Having breathed the Holy Spirit on them, he authorizes the disciples to remit or retain peoples' sins (20:23). What

does this mean so far as the understanding of sin is concerned in this Gospel? In other words, how does the theme of revelation fit with the charge?

34. "My God": Jesus & Thomas

Jesus to Mary (20:17)	Thomas to Jesus (20:28)
1.	My Lord
2. My God	My God
3. & your (pl.) God	
4. My Father (2x)	
5. & your (pl.) Father	

1. Thomas' confession is often cited as yet another proof—this time at the Gospel's climax—that John believed Jesus to have been divine in the manner later formulated by classic Christian doctrine.

2. However, Jesus' own earlier declaration to Mary Magdalene is rarely attended to by such apologists. Yet, is it not in keeping with what was so apparent throughout the Gospel, but vividly demonstrated in 5:17–30 (FP 16): that, in his incarnate state (as distinct from his status as Son within the Trinity), Jesus was fully subservient to the Father?

3. See Revelation 3:12 (by the same author?) for other instances of the expression—in this case occurring three times in a single verse.

35. Two Pentecosts?

	John 20:19–23	Acts 2:1–38
1. Who? (source)	[Father (16:16, 26)]	Father (33)
2. Who? (agent)	Jesus	Jesus (33)
3. What? (event #1)	Breathes Holy Spirit	Pours out Holy Spirit (33)
4. What? (event #2)	Forgive/retain sins	Forgiveness promised/received (38)
5. Whom? (subject)	Disciples (Twelve?)	Twelve, disciples, pilgrims (1–11)
6. Where? (place)	Jerusalem (private)	Jerusalem (private-public)
7. When? (time #1)	Post-resurrection	Post-resurrection (1)
8. When? (time #2)	Pre-ascension	Post-ascension (1)

1. Are the similarities sufficiently numerous and significant to suggest that this is one and the same event, told in John's (by now) familiar and distinctive way?

2. Are the differences sufficiently numerous and significant to suggest that these are two separate occasions: an early, anticipatory, private one; and a later, fuller, public one? The answer may in part depend on a prior commitment to a certain kind of confession-based historicism: that the inerrancy of Scripture demands that one harmonize the accounts or distinguish them in a before-after mode.

3. Christians have been divided over whether the Spirit proceeds from the Father (Eastern church) or from the Father and the Son (Western church)—the distinctions having implications for Trinitarian doctrine. There are biblical statements that support each of the alternatives. Some Orthodox theologians have suggested that the controversy might be resolved on the basis of an interpretation proposed by St. Maximus the Confessor: from the Father, through the Son (Breck, p. 176). This would have the support of texts such as Acts 2:33.

36. John & the Synoptics: A Fresh Look?

Basic Distinctions	Synoptics	John
1. The Public Message	Kingdom of the Age to Come	Life of the Age to Come
(FP 1, 11)		
2. Restrained Christology	Son of God, Messiah	Equal/one with Father
(FP 1, 20)	(Silencing demons & disciples)	(Submitting to Father)
3. Relating to Jesus	Receiving the Sender	Believing in the Sender
(FP 1, 26)	(Mark 9:37)	(12:44)

Although I deliberately avoided raising historical issues, believing that these would distract from a direct encounter with the text of the FG as we have it, here are some matters that ought to be considered should further study be taken up.

1. We saw in FP 1 that, despite the dramatic discoveries bringing about the New Look on the FG, there remained three areas of apparently fundamental distinctiveness (the leftmost column above) that were largely unaffected by the new paleographic and archaeological finds of the 1930s and 40s.

2. However, in FP 11, 20, and 26, I proposed fresh ways of seeing the existing internal evidence of the SG and FG that might warrant another kind of Second Look. They are brought together here:

   a. With regard to "the public message" of Jesus, the textual evidence from Mark 10:17–27 suggests that inheriting eternal/aeonic life, entering the kingdom of God, and being saved are equivalent terms for the same reality—the choice of expressions being determined by one or more of several circumstances.

   b. So far as "restrained Christology" is concerned, we saw that (ironically), in the two places where Jesus, according to John, is most declarative about his unity and equality with the Father

(5:17–30 and 10:29–37), he is most insistent upon underscoring his obedient and dependent sonship. This restraint (even a kind of redefinition) corresponds to Jesus' regular silencing of the demons when they address him in exalted titles (Mark 1–3) and when he forbids his disciples to tell of his identity as the Messiah—shifting instead to the suffering, dying, and rising Son of Man (Mark 8:27–33).

c. Finally, "relating to Jesus" as the ultimate goal is denied by Jesus himself. Rather, one's aim is to receive (Mark 9:37) or believe in the Sender (John 12:44). The latter claim ("He cried out") is made in Jerusalem at the climax of the public ministry.

3. This approach might be viewed as special pleading for the historicity of both Gospel traditions (e.g., "John and the Synoptics are really saying the same thing 'in other words'; and this corresponds to historical reality.") unless it is borne out by other data (explicit and implied) and by a consensus about what constitutes historical reasoning.

Appendix

Cleanthes' *Hymn to Zeus*[*]

Noblest of immortals, many-named, always all-powerful
Zeus, first cause and ruler of nature, governing everything with your law,
greetings! For it is right for all mortals to address you:
for we have our origin in you, bearing a likeness to God,

5   we, alone of all that live and move as mortal creatures on earth.
Therefore, I shall praise you constantly; indeed I always sing of your rule.
This whole universe, spinning around the earth, truly
obeys you wherever you lead, and is readily ruled by you;
such a servant do you have between your unconquerable hands,

10   the two-edged, fiery, ever-living thunderbolt.
For by its stroke all works of nature <are guided>.
With it you direct the universal reason, which permeates
everything, mingling with the great and the small lights.
Because of this you are so great, the highest king for ever.

15   Not a single thing takes place on earth without you, God,
nor in the divine celestial sphere nor in the sea,
except what bad people do in their folly.
But you know how to make the uneven even
and to put into order the disorderly; even the unloved is dear to you.

20   For you have thus joined everything into one, the good with the bad,

---

* Translated by Johan C. Thom.

that there comes to be one ever-existing rational order for everything.

This all mortals that are bad flee and avoid,

the wretched, who though always desiring to acquire good things,

neither see nor hear God's universal law,

25   obeying which they could have a good life with understanding.

But they on the contrary rush without regard to the good, each after different things,

some with a belligerent eagerness for glory,

others without discipline intent on profits,

others yet on indulgence and the pleasurable actions of the body.

30   <They desire the good,> but they are borne now to this, then to that,

while striving eagerly that the complete opposite of these things happen.

But all-bountiful Zeus, cloud-wrapped ruler of the thunderbolt,

deliver human beings from their destructive ignorance;

disperse it from their souls; grant that they obtain

35   the insight on which you rely when governing everything with justice;

so that we, having been honored, may honor you in return,

constantly praising your works, as befits

one who is mortal. For there is no other greater privilege for mortals

or for gods than always to praise the universal law in justice.

Bibliography

Barrett, C. K., editor. *The New Testament Background: Selected Documents*. New York: Harper, 1961. Fragment of Cleanthes' *Hymn to Zeus*, p. 63.

Bowker, John. "The Son of Man." *JTS* 28 (1977) 19–48.

Boyarin, Daniel. *The Jewish Gospels: The Story of the Jewish Christ*. New York: New Press, 2012.

Breck, John. *Scripture in Tradition: The Bible and Its Interpretation in the Orthodox Church*. Crestwood, NY: St. Vladimir's Seminary Press, 2001.

Bultmann, Rudolf. *Theology of the New Testament*. Translated by Kendrick Grobel. 2 vols. New York: Scribner, 1951–55.

Burridge, Richard A. *Four Gospels, One Jesus?: A Symbolic Reading*. Grand Rapids: Eerdmans, 1994. See pp. 131–66.

Caird, George. *A Commentary on the Revelation of St. John the Divine*. HNTC. NY: Harper & Row, 1966.

Cartlidge, David R., and David L. Dungan, editors. *Documents for the Study of the Gospels*. Rev. ed. Minneapolis: Fortress, 1994.

Chapman, Stephen. "A Brazen Faith." *Ex Auditu* 16 (2000) 187–91.

Charlesworth, James H., editor. *John and the Dead Sea Scrolls*. Christian Origins Library. New York: Crossroad, 1990.

Dodd, C. H. *Historical Tradition in the Fourth Gospel*. Cambridge, England: University Press, 1963.

Fuglseth, Kåre Sigvald. *Johannine Sectarianism in Perspective: A Social, Historical, and Comparative Analysis of Temple and Social Relationships in the Gospel of John, Philo, and Qumran*. NovTSup 119. Boston: Brill, 2005. See pp. 1–65.

Harvey, A. E. *Jesus and the Constraints of History*. Bampton Lectures 1980. London: Duckworth, 1982.

Hase, Karl von. *Geschichte Jesu*. 2nd ed. Leipzig: Breitkopf und Härtel, 1876.

Holmes, Arthur F. *All Truth Is God's Truth*. Downers Grove, IL: InterVarsity, 1977.

Hoskyns, Edwyn Clement. *The Fourth Gospel*. Edited by Francis Noel Davey. 2nd ed. London: Faber, 1947.

Kee, Howard Clark. *The New Testament in Context. Sources and Documents*. Englewood Cliffs, NJ: Prentice-Hall, 1984. Inscriptions to Asclepios, pp. 144–46; fragment of Cleanthes' *Hymn to Zeus*, p. 225.

Lee, Dorothy A. *Flesh and Glory: Symbolism, Gender, and Theology in the Gospel of John*. New York: Crossroad, 2002.

Lemcio, Eugene E. "Father and Son in the Synoptics and John." In *The New Testament as Canon: A Reader in Canonical Criticism*, edited by Robert W. Wall and Eugene E. Lemcio, 67–77. Sheffield: Sheffield Academic, 1992.

————. *Navigating Revelation: Charts for the Voyage. A Pedagogical Aid.* Eugene, OR: Wipf and Stock, 2011.

————. "'Son of Man,' 'Pitiable Man,' 'Rejected Man': Equivalent Expressions in the Old Greek of Daniel." *TynBul* 56/1 (2005) 43–60.

————. "The Synoptics and John: The Two So Long Divided. Hearing Canonical Voices for Ecclesial Conversations." *HBT* 26/1 (June 2004) 50–96. Because publishing this journal had transferred hands, and because sufficient care was not taken to ensure electronic correspondence with the Greek program used originally, the text omits footnote 3 and contains a jumble of accents and breathings, for which the editor apologized in the next number.

————. *Travels with St. Mark: GPS for the Journey. A Pedagogical Aid.* Eugene, OR: Wipf and Stock, 2012.

Levine, Amy-Jill. *The Misunderstood Jew: The Church and the Scandal of the Jewish Jesus.* San Francisco: Harper, 2006.

Maloney, F. J. "Recent Johannine Studies: Part Two: Monographs." *ExpTim* 123/9 (June 2012) 417–28.

Moule, C. F. D. "The Individualism of the Fourth Gospel." *NovT* 5 (1962) 171–90. Reprinted in his *Essays in New Testament Interpretation*, 91–109. Cambridge: University Press, 1982.

O'Day, Gail R. *Revelation in the Fourth Gospel: Narrative Mode and Theological Claim.* Philadelphia: Fortress, 1986.

Outler, Albert C., translator and editor. *Augustine: Confessions and Enchiridion.* Louisville: Westminster John Knox, 2006.

Pietersma, Albert, and Benjamin E. Wright, editors. *A New English Translation of the Septuagint* [NETS]. New York: Oxford University Press, 2007.

Plantinga, Cornelius. "Christ, the Snake." *Perspectives* 6 (March 1991) 14–15.

Robinson, John A. T. *The Priority of John.* Edited by J. F. Coakley. London: SCM, 1985. See pp. 325–29.

Southwell, Robert. "A Child, My Choice." In *Collected Poems* by Southwell, edited by Peter Davidson and Anne Sweeney, 12. Manchester: Carcanet, 2007.

Thom, Johan C. *Cleanthes' Hymn to Zeus: Text, Translation, and Commentary.* STAC 33. Tübingen: Mohr Siebeck, 2005.

Traina, Robert A. *Methodical Bible Study: A New Approach to Hermeneutics.* New York: Biblical Seminary, 1952.

Vermes, Geza, translator and editor. *The Complete Dead Sea Scrolls in English.* London: Penguin, 2003.

Wilder, Amos N. *Theopoetic: Theology and the Religious Imagination.* Philadelphia: Fortress, 1976.

Williams, Charles. *The Figure of Beatrice: A Study of Dante.* London: Faber & Faber, 1943.

Wrede, William. *Das Messiasgeheimnis in den Evangelien: Zugleich ein Beitrag zum Verständnis des Markusevangeliums.* Göttingen: Vandenhoeck & Ruprecht, 1901. English translation published as *The Messianic Secret.* Translated by J. C. G. Grieg. Library of Theological Translations. London: Clarke, 1971.